SOCIAL MEDIA TIP'S AND TRICKS -2

PAWAN KUMAR BHAT

Copyright © Pawan Kumar Bhat
All Rights Reserved.

ISBN 978-1-63873-392-8

This book has been published with all efforts taken to make the material error-free after the consent of the author. However, the author and the publisher do not assume and hereby disclaim any liability to any party for any loss, damage, or disruption caused by errors or omissions, whether such errors or omissions result from negligence, accident, or any other cause.

While every effort has been made to avoid any mistake or omission, this publication is being sold on the condition and understanding that neither the author nor the publishers or printers would be liable in any manner to any person by reason of any mistake or omission in this publication or for any action taken or omitted to be taken or advice rendered or accepted on the basis of this work. For any defect in printing or binding the publishers will be liable only to replace the defective copy by another copy of this work then available.

Contents

1. Chapter 1 — 1
2. Chapter 2 — 9

CHAPTER ONE

By now, you're no stranger to the fact that social media is a powerful tool for business, both on and offline. Whether you're brand new to the Internet marketing game, or you're looking to learn more about how to leverage social media to enhance your business, this book is for you.

Benefits of Using Social Media to Internet Marketers

Social media marketing carries many benefits to Internet marketers, including:

ESTABLISHING A BRAND AND RAISING AWARENESS

The majority of people on the Internet today are using at least one social media network, such as Facebook, Twitter, or Google+. A good bit of them are using two, or even all three of those social networks. Getting your brand out there on those platforms is a good way to let people know you're around.

SPYING ON THE COMPETITION

By following your competition, you can see what kind of deals they are offering customers, and keep up to date with other things they have going on. Just be sure that whatever you have to offer is better.

CONDUCTING MARKET RESEARCH

Social media can help you listen to what your customers have to say about your products or services. By tracking what they click on and what they avoid, you can see what your customers like and are responding to. People will share their thoughts and opinions on social media websites, so you can use the information to your advantage.

ENHANCED CUSTOMER LOYALTY AND TRUST

Social media allows you to speak to your customers on a more personal level, which makes them feel more important to you, and more valued. In turn, customers are more likely to trust you, which means they are more likely to do business with you, instead of the competition.

INTERACTING WITH YOUR AUDIENCE

People visit social media websites for the interaction with their peers, not to be bombarded with ads. This allows you to pitch your products and interact with your audience in much more authentic way. You can use the platform to ask customers to share their thoughts and opinions, which makes them feel like you're listening, and you end up being real connections and relationships with your customers.

BRINGING ATTENTION TO YOUR PRODUCT OR SERVICE

Social media moves at lightening speed. If you want to promote your product, doing so on social media is one of the quickest ways to get attention to it. If you offer a money saving promotion, it's even better because your sales will skyrocket!

HIGHER QUALITY CUSTOMER SERVICE

Social media platforms allow you to address customer concerns directly, and in a timely manner. When a customer doesn't have to wait hours to get the answers they need *and* they get a personal touch, they will be more satisfied, which means you'll have better customer service. And, you'll be able to save money on toll-free lines and long distance fees.

ESTABLISHING YOURSELF AS AN EXPERT

If you're passionate about a certain topic—whether it's your professional field or a hobby, the Internet can help you establish yourself as an expert by giving you a platform to share information. People will be coming to you for information on the topic, and telling their friends about you.

BUILDING YOUR PERSONAL REPUTATION

Social media allows you to get your name out there, and talk about the various things that matter to you. This is key to building a good online reputation, which is critical if you intend to find a job or make new business connections.

BUILDING AND ENHANCING PERSONAL AND PROFESSIONAL RELATIONSHIPS

Social media allows you to build and enhance both personal and professional relationships. You can use it to connect with other industry experts, or find old friends from high school you're looking to reconnect with.

SHARING INFORMATION WITH LIKE-MINDED PEOPLE

Distance is no longer a barrier. You can connect with professionals in your field that are in the same city, or across the globe, as if they were next door neighbors.

Facebook vs. Twitter vs. Google+

It can be hard to decide where to market, and how to market to your customers with Internet marketing. Of course, we're making it a bit easier on you by dedicating a chapter in this book to each of these social media powerhouse networks, but before we get ahead of ourselves let's do a quick comparison of
each of the networks, so you can understand where they are alike and where they are different, to truly understand their value to you as an Internet Marketer.

FACEBOOK

Strengths

- **Critical Mass:** Facebook is the largest social media network, and often competes with Google as the most trafficked website on the Internet. Many people joined because so many other people and businesses they know are already on the platform. At last count, there were more than 750 million users—and the thing that makes this so important is they don't just use the site—they use it often, and when they do, they stick around for a while.
- **Keeping Up with Everyone:** Keep up with what's going on with everyone in your life—friends, family, acquaintances, and business connections.
- **Brand Promotion:** When someone "likes" your business Facebook page, they are essentially advertising it to their friends for you.
- **InternalAnalytics:**Facebook includes data about how users interact with your page and how many users see the information right from within its dashboard.

Ease of Engagement: Users can share an opinion about something with the click of a button. That one click advertises an item to the users entire social circle, with additional comment being optional.

Weaknesses

- **Segmenting Your Life:** There's no easy way to separate contacts from your personal and professional life. Google+ has this covered with its Circles feature, which we'll discuss later in this book.

- **Privacy:** Facebook's privacy settings and mechanisms are constantly changing—without announcement at that. Without staying up-to-date on how to protect your information from prying eyes, the best thing you can do is assume everything you say or do on the platform is public.

Environment: Facebook is known for its old interface style, though they are currently undergoing some changes to bring it more current. Facebook still, despite its high usage level, has a low satisfaction rate. While we're not ready to say it's going become another MySpace, it's certainly worth mentioning the battle with Google+.

TWITTER

Strengths

- **Following Interests:** Through the use of hastags (#hashtag), Twitter makes it exceptionally easy to follow topics and issues without actually following the people in the conversation. This way you can keep up with hot button issues in your industry.

Brevity: The character limit is ideal for short attention spans, so people can quickly scan for the information they need.

Weaknesses

- **Brevity:** While some love it, the 140-character limit can be frustrating because it's hard to whittle down important points.
- **Information Overload:** If you have a large following, there's potential to miss a lot. With frequent tweets, you're going to see a lot stream by fast, which is enough to overload you, quickly.

- **Platform:** While Twitter has made improvements, the system does overload and shut down from time to time. Even though it's temporary, sometimes only lasting a few seconds, it's frustrating.

Internal Analytics: There is a lack of internal analytics data available for you to see.

GOOGLE+

Strengths

- **Segmenting Your Life**: Easily keep your family separate from your friends, and your work contacts separate from your personal life.
- **Video Chats and Hangouts:** Meet face-to-face without ever leaving your living room or office!

Integration with Other Google Services: Google+ fits right in with all their other services, including search and maps.

Weaknesses

- **Difficult to Scan**: The home screen of Google+ is difficult to scan. As you add more people to your circles, you'll have to scroll more and more to be able to keep up with what is going on.
- **Lack of Brevity**: While the lack of a limit on status update length is nice for some, others will abuse the privilege, making it that much more difficult to scan and digest information.
- **Lack of Critical Mass:** While Google+ is gaining ground every day, there's still nowhere near as many people there as there is on Facebook or Twitter.

Why Use It? As the Google+ platform becomes more clearly defined, the answer to this question will arise. Many marketers see great potential and use it to their advantage, while others are still wondering what it really has to offer. We'll cover it more thoroughly its own chapter, so you can decide for yourself.

Now that we've covered the basic strengths and weaknesses of each social media platform we're covering in this book, let's dive right in and take a closer look at how to make them work for you.

CHAPTER TWO

What it is

Twitter is one of the most popular social networking platforms on the Internet today. It is considered a micro-blogging platform, as there is a limit on the number of characters you can use in each update. It can be used to communicate with people you know, to develop connections with people you want to know, and to keep up to date with the latest trends. Internet marketers use it to drive traffic to their websites, and engage with customers.

Benefits to Internet Marketers

RESEARCH

With the use of hashtags making it easy to research nearly any topic imaginable, the built in search feature is a valuable research tool. While the functionality will not replace the competitive research tools out there on the market today, it can help gather information about what's hot in the market, and where needs are within a particular niche.

DRIVE TRAFFIC TO YOUR WEBSITE

Many people will tweet their new blog posts out to their followers. However, just tweeting about your new blog post doesn't mean people will listen and click. For this to work, you need to be actively involved in the network, and sharing valuable information your network is interested in or is looking for.

ENGAGE WITH CUSTOMERS

Businesses can communicate with their customer base, and get feedback in a causal, and cost effective way. Find out what your customers love (or hate) about what you have to offer, and make changes to improve it for them.

NETWORKING

Twitter enables you to connect and communicate with friends and family, but it can also be a powerful professional networking tool. In addition, it can be a great way for employees within the same organization to communicate back and forth because it is so short and to the point.

BRANDING

Matching your Twitter handle to your business name, and using custom graphics on your Twitter profile can be a great way to reinforce your brand, and to help raise awareness in its early stages.

Getting Followers

- **Make sure what you post has value.** People will ignore you if it's garbage.
- **Use hashtags.** This categorizes what you're talking about, which makes it easier for people to find.
- **Tweet on topic most of the time.** At least 80% of the time, talk about your business niche. This helps establish your credibility.
- **Make use of your profile space.** Describe who you are, and link to your website.

- **Link to your profile from other social media profiles.** This helps people see that you are on Twitter.
- **Include your Twitter link in your email signature.** This too, helps people see that you are on Twitter.
- **Advertise your twitter link on your business cards.** This helps with offline marketing efforts and may bring additional followers.
- **Use Twitter search.** Find people who you want to connect with. See who's talking about what, and jump in the conversation.
- **Use @s.** @twitterhandle lets you engage a person directly. Do this often!

- **Use Follow Friday (#FF)** Not only will this help you suggest other people to your followers, you may find some awesome new connections this way.

Follow Friends of Friends. This can help you find other relevant followers to engage.

Making Tweets

- **Use a URL shortener.** Something like bit.ly or owl.ly will shorten your URL to save you characters in your tweet, and it'll help you track the number of times it was clicked.
- **Share information of value.** Whether it's yours or not, share something you think your followers can use. You'll get more respect when you're not tooting your own horn all the time!

Use HootSuite or something similar. Programs such as HootSuite and TweetDeck will allow you better manage your social media efforts. You can track several things on one screen, and even schedule tweets ahead of time, so you don't actually have to be in front of the screen to share

information. Just be sure you're actively communicating with people who respond to your tweets—don't set and forget!

With the two veteran social networks out of the way, let's take a look at the newcomer to the market, Google+.

www.ingramcontent.com/pod-product-compliance
Lightning Source LLC
Chambersburg PA
CBHW021002180526
45163CB00006B/2471